Let's Be Thankful

P. K. Hallinan

ideals children's books

Nashville, Tennessee

ISBN-13: 978-0-8249-5604-2

Published by Ideals Children's Books
An imprint of Ideals Publications
A Guideposts Company
Nashville, Tennessee
www.idealsbooks.com

Color separations by Precision Color Graphics, Franklin, Wisconsin
Printed and bound in the United States of America

Library of Congress CIP data on file

Designed by Georgina Chidlow-Rucker

10 9 8 7 6 5 4 3 2 1

This book is for

_____

◆ ◆ ◆

From

_____

I like to be thankful for all I receive,
From the tiniest seashell . . .

To the mightiest breeze.

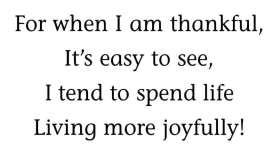

For when I am thankful,
It's easy to see,
I tend to spend life
Living more joyfully!

So, I'm thankful for small things,
Like bugs on the ground . . .

And warm little puppies
That follow me around.

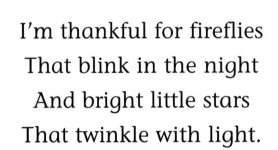

I'm thankful for fireflies
That blink in the night
And bright little stars
That twinkle with light.

I like to be thankful for bigger things too—
Like seeing a sunrise . . .

Or a trip to the zoo!

But also I'm thankful for everyday things,
Like a nice scoop of ice cream . . .

Or just swinging on swings!

I'm thankful for lemonade to sip from a glass.

I'm thankful for baseball and thick, wavy grass.

And I'm thankful for others,
Who help me so much,
Like firemen and policemen
And soldiers, and such.

I'm thankful for my teachers
And all that they give.

I'm thankful for my country—
What a great place to live!

But mostly I'm thankful for my family and friends,
Who make me so happy . . .

Whose love never ends.
And when all's said and done, it seems very clear . . .

I like to be thankful
For just being here.